Look at My Book

How Kids Can Write & Illustrate Terrific Books

written and illustrated by

Loreen Leedy

SCHOLASTIC INC.
New York Toronto London Auckland Sydney
Mexico City New Delhi Hong Kong Buenos Aires

ISBN 0-439-69998-3

Published by Scholastic Inc., 557 Broadway, New York, NY 10012, by arrangement with Holiday House, Inc.

12 11 10 9 8 7 6 5 4 3 7 8 9/0

Printed in the U.S.A. 40

First Scholastic printing, September 2004

Dear Young Authors and Artists,

Have you ever made your own book? This book is full of ideas you can use when you write and illustrate your own stories. Use it as a general guide, and please ask a grown-up for help if you need it. When I start a book, I grab a pencil and some paper....Let's get going!

Loreen Leedy

Ideas

The words and art in a book start with ideas.

Books are full of ideas!

TIPS on getting ideas:

Read.

Ask questions.

Learn something new.

Listen to what people say.

Watch the world around you.

Think of how to improve things.

Invent an imaginary world.

Remember details.

Keep a journal.

Doodle.

And don't forget to . . .

I want to write about birds, but I need more ideas.

Brainstorming

means to think of a whole bunch of ideas.

Brainstorming TIPS:

1) Make a list of your ideas.
2) Make an idea web.
3) Draw pictures.
4) Try to think of as many ideas as possible.
5) Think of weird ideas, boring ideas, silly ideas—a "bad" idea might lead to a great one.
6) Try brainstorming with another person or a group.
7) Write down each idea so you don't forget it.

Genres are different types of books.
What genres are there?
Let's go to the library and see.
Can I go? Can I go?
Would you like to write a fairy tale? Or a mystery? Or a how-to book? Or a joke book?
Once upon
Fiction
Science Fiction
Fantasy
Mystery
The Aliens Amon Us
Look at all these different kinds of books.
I wonder if I could write an adventure story?
The Fairy Ring
Fai ales
Myths
LOST IN THE JUNGLE
Adventur
Tall Tales

Research
means to look for information.
Why are you reading about swamps?
I might put one in my book.
SWAMPS OF THE WORLD
Swamp Survival
Swamps A to Z
To find information to use in your book, look here:
videos
books
the Internet
magazines
almanacs
encyclopedias
ask an expert
newspapers
CDs
Owls of the Americas
HOOPLA
How to Play Basketball
History
Poetry
Humor
Sports
Travel
Nature
How-to
Science
I need to find out more about birds.
ABOUT BIRDS
That's my Uncle Arf!
Famous Dogs
Famous Dogs
Gnu Jokes

Characters can be real or imaginary.

can be people, animals, or something else....

What traits does each character have?
You look happy.
I think he'll be curious. And daring. And brilliant.
Let's see—I'm cheerful, brave, smart, athletic, energetic...
It's a sunny day!
I Hate Mornings!
Some TRAITS:
Young or Old
Neat or Sloppy
Silly or Serious
Nice or Mean
Tall or Short
Juicy or Dry
Think of a name for each fictional character you invent.
My name is Snookums.
I've got to think of just the right name for my character.
How about Jon? Or Jack? Jake? Zeke?
How about Zak?
I'm
Esme.
My designation is X2PODiP-E. Who are you?
Hi, I'm Zoomer.

Setting is the time and place your story happens.

WHERE could your book take place?

Inside a teacup?

On the moon?

In a stone castle?

On a tropical island?

Under your bed?

On the bottom of a lake?

When I was six months old,
I rode on a fire truck.
I guess every place
I've ever been could be
a setting for my book.
On my first birthday
I went to the circus.
Last summer I was
in the sky in a
hot-air balloon.
I was in Paris last week.
WHEN could your book take place?
At dawn?
During summer vacation?
At midnight?
During prehistoric times?
When your grandfather was a baby?
Before electricity was invented?
In the future?

Plan

Make a plan to guide you as you "build" your book.

Start to imagine what could be in your book.

Make a list of what might be in your book.

Title (Lindy's Birds?)
About the Author
Dedication
Penguins
Ducks
Ostriches
Hummingbirds
Cardinals
Owls
Toucans

Make a **storyboard** to plan the sequence of events. (It looks a lot like a comic strip.)

Try out different plans for your book. Which one do you like best?

Zak leaves for vaca
He goes on a hike.
He gets lost in the
A wild pig runs a
He hides in a cav
He finds a circle
He lifts up a bi
A rusty can is
It's full of old
Zak buys a boat
terrible weather, gets home.

Zak flies over a wilderness.
The fuel tank starts to leak.
He lands and starts walking.
He suddenly falls into a sinkhole.
A big bear skeleton falls on him.
He starts to dig himself out.
He finds an old gold coin.
He digs and digs for more.
He finds a wooden box.
It won't open, but it's heavy.
He takes it home and opens it.
It's full of worthless rocks.

Fiction Writing TIPS:

1) When you're writing a story, you need a good **plot**. (The plot is "what happens.") Give your story a beginning, a middle, and an end.
2) In most stories, the main character has a **problem**. What problem can you give to your character?
3) What **solution** is there? Get your character in trouble, then help him or her get out of trouble again.

Nonfiction Writing TIPS:

1) Nonfiction is based on **facts**. Find facts to include by doing research (see page 7).
2) Some ways to do research:
   Interview an expert.
   Visit a place in person.
   Watch an event.
   Look in books, CDs, videos, etc.
   Search on the Internet.
3) Take **notes** on what you find out. Also, take photographs and/or make sketches.

Rough draft

Your first try at writing the text for your book.

TIPS for rough drafts:

1) Use your notes, lists, and plans to get started.
2) Write quickly. Don't try to get everything perfect at this stage.
3) Leave plenty of space between each line so you can scribble in new words as you go.
4) Have fun and experiment with your writing. You can always change any part of it later on.

Rough Sketches

The first step in making the art for your book.

TIPS for rough sketches:

1) Find a picture of the subject to use as a guide while you're drawing (optional).
2) Make simple line drawings of the characters and settings you plan to use. Don't try to make final art, just loose sketches for now.
3) Draw with short, light strokes. Don't press down on your pencil too hard.

Have you thought of a good title yet?
Title
Give your book an interesting title.
Zak and the Gator?
The Swamp Treasure?
Muddy Millions?
Zak's Treasure Hunt?
All About Me?
My Fabulous Life?
A Dog's Tail?
The Life of a Dog?
Best in Show
The Best Birds?
The Birds I Love?
My Favorite Birds?
Beautiful Birds?
?
A Book by Me
Hoots
Ten Funny Owl Stories
Title TIPS:
1) A good title makes people want to read your book.
2) The title should tell readers what your book is about.
3) If your book needs it, add a subtitle (an extra title after the main one).
The Sixteenth Page

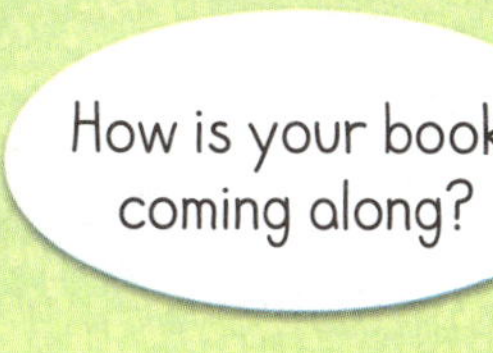

Share what you have so far and get suggestions.

Zak dropped some nuts. The gator wouldn't leave.

Why don't you put a dog in your story?

The dog could sniff out the treasure and dig it up and chase the gator and...

Maybe Zak gets lost for days and has to eat lizards and spiders!

What if after Zak finds the treasure, the gator eats it?

I like some of these ideas but not all of them.

Sharing TIPS:

1) Show your rough drafts and sketches to one person or a group.
2) Ask for ideas and suggestions about how you can make your book better.
3) Use the suggestions you like and make changes to your book.
4) If you don't like someone's idea, just ignore it.

Revise means to rewrite.

Revising TIPS:

1) Add words and take out words.
2) Switch words around.
3) Use lively language.
4) Use specific words instead of general words.
5) Include interesting details.
6) Brainstorm again if you need to.
7) Do more research if you need to.

My Favorite Birds by Lindy

~~What~~ Which birds live on ice and fly in ~~water~~ the ocean? Penguins! The biggest ones are emperor~~s~~ penguins. They live in Antarctica. The female lays one egg at a time. The male keeps it warm until it hatches. Penguins ~~swim in~~ dive into the ocean to catch fish and shrimp to eat.

Zak's Muddy Treasure by Jason

It was a hot sticky day. ~~The~~ Sweat ~~ran~~ dripped off Zak's face. He paddled his ~~boat~~ canoe in the dark water. "~~Why did I come~~ What am I doing here?" he thought. ~~One~~ A week before, Zak went to a used book store. He ~~looked in~~ opened an old book and a map fell out. It was from

means to fix mistakes.

Editing is scary!

It doesn't have to be.

I can help check spelling.

So can I.

That should be a capital O.

That sentence needs a period at the end.

A Dog's Life by Harrison Fuzz

My first memery is of my mother lick
my face. Her ~~tung~~ tongue was like a huge w
beach towel. sometimes when sh
it felt like I was drowning.

It took me only week to learn h
wag my tail Dad was so proud!
yip the loudist and bite hardist, t
sisters used to hide ~~on~~ under the bed.

One of the scaryest things we had to
learn was how to walk down stair
one time I really hurt my leg
I still limp a little when it rains The other

Format

is the size and shape of your book.

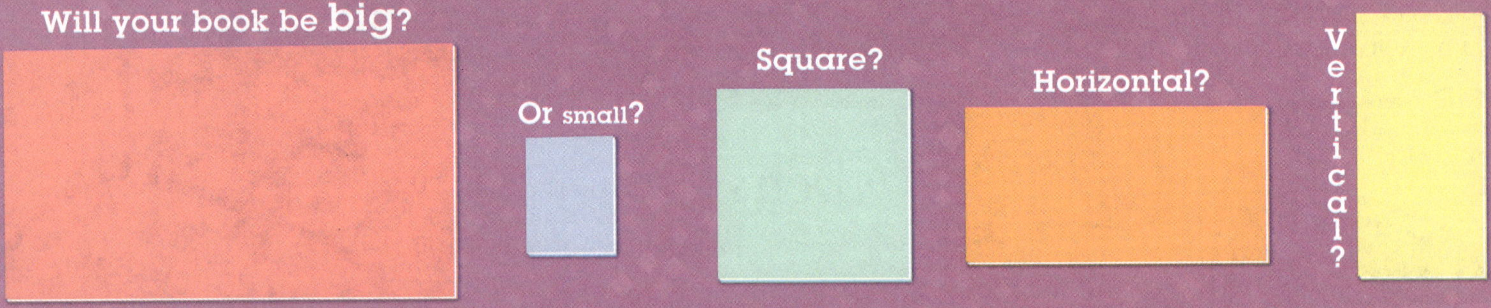

Will your book be **big**?

Or small?

Square?

Horizontal?

Vertical?

Will your book have an interesting shape? (Keep the shape simple so it's easy to turn the pages.)

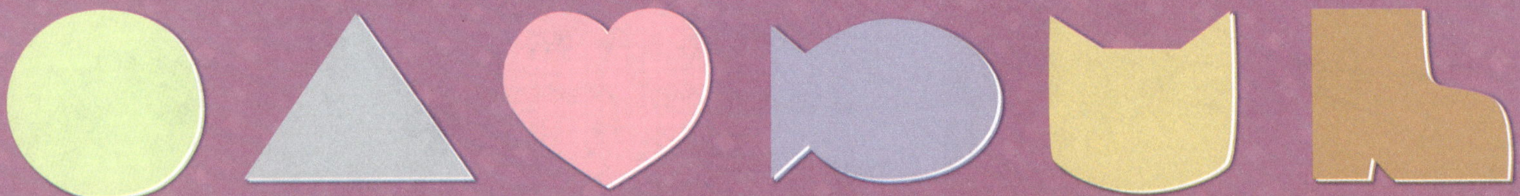

This looks like an alligator head, I think.

Try making a scroll.

Or make a zigzag-shaped book.

Your book could have flaps.

Or pockets.

Or pop-ups.

Layout

Sketch a design to figure out where the words and art will go on the pages.

One simple layout for a two-page spread is to put the words on one page and the art on the other.

Layout TIPS:

1) Write out the words by hand or use a computer printout to see how much space they take up.
2) Try putting the lines of words inside the art or curving them around the art.

A **book plan** has layouts for all the pages of your book.

back cover front cover

title page

spread

Your book can include one or more of these special pages:

Title page	Author page	Copyright	Dedication	Contents	Resources	Glossary
An Amazing Story written and illustrated by Arthur Arteeste	Your Name Age Town A Photograph Interests etc.	©2010 by Your Name (use current year)	(For example:) This book is dedicated to my Uncle Arf, who taught me how to howl.	Penguins 2–3 Toucans 4 Ducks 5 Hummingbirds 6 Owls 7 Ostriches 8 Cardinals 9 About the Author 10	(Make a list of books, websites, videos, clubs, magazines, and other sources for readers to get more information.)	Glossary: a list of key words in your book with definitions

Pick a style for your book.

Lines

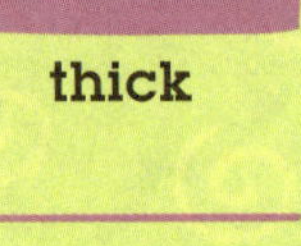

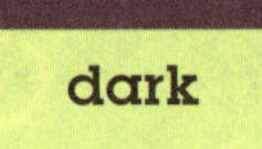

thick · smooth · jagged · dotted · lumpy · dark

thin · sketchy · wiggly · dashed · soft · light

Shapes

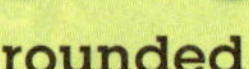

average · skinny · plump · rounded · distorted

Patterns

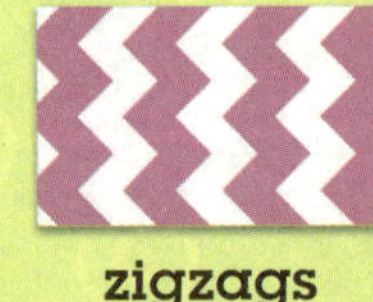

spots · checks · stripes · plaid · waves · zigzags

The lines, shapes, colors, and so on create the style of your book's **illustrations**.

Art brings your book to life.

Illustration TIPS:

1) Gather your text, sketches, and layouts.
2) Test your art supplies and paper. Use paper for your book's pages that works well with the art supplies. For example, paint watercolors on heavy paper.
3) Cut the paper to the size of your book's pages. Or work on larger paper and cut it to size later.
4) Lightly sketch in art and words with pencil. See page 28 for lettering ideas.
5) Apply art supplies (next page). Allow artwork to dry.
6) Erase any sketch lines that show.

There are many different art supplies you can use for your book's illustrations.

Lettering can be plain or decorative.

Lettering TIPS:

1) Use decorative letters for the title and plainer letters for the text.
2) Lightly draw in the letters with a pencil. Go over the lines with a gel pen, marker, or other tool.

Plain TALL Swirly wide ANGLED

Dotty Rough Flowery melting Spooky

Thorny Blobby wiggly holes Square

holds a book's pages together.

Here are four easy ways to bind your book.

Yummy!

My Garden Visitors by Ann Kim

1) Measure and mark each hole. Each page needs at least two holes.

2) Make holes in one page at a time with a hole punch.

3) Tie pages and covers together with a shoelace, yarn, or string.

1) Gather the covers and pages. Line them up by tapping gently.

2) Staple in a straight row along the left edge.

1) Make a blank book by folding sheets of plain paper in half. Staple down the crease.

2) Attach art and text to each page with glue or tape.

1) Punch holes in pages with a 3-hole punch.

2) Insert pages into a folder that has built-in paper fasteners.

3) Spread open paper fasteners to hold pages securely.

Examples

The possibilities are ENDLESS!

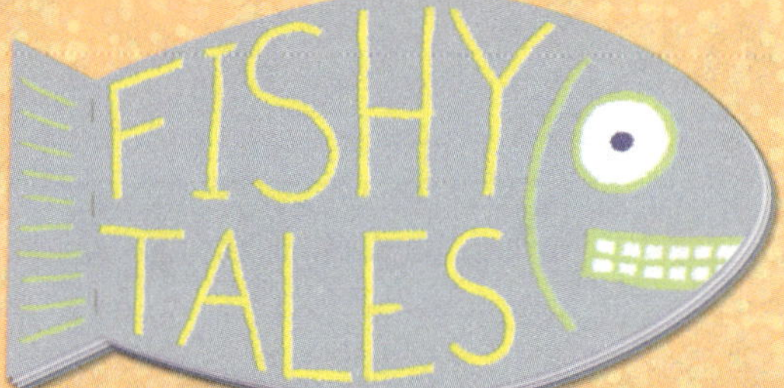

Don't Eat the Mystery Meat!
Advice for New Students

Look at my book!

OWLS

10 Ways to Lose a Friend

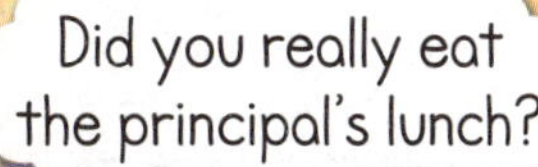

To find out more about making books, try looking here:

Learning to Write and Illustrate

Bang, Molly. ***Picture This: How Pictures Work.*** SeaStar Books, 2000. A professional illustrator shows how shapes and colors create a mood and tell a story.

Bauer, Marion Diane. ***What's Your Story? A Young Person's Guide to Writing Fiction.*** Clarion Books, 1992.

Christelow, Eileen. ***What Do Illustrators Do?*** Houghton Mifflin Co., 1997. Two artists use different art styles to illustrate the same story.
What Do Writers Do? Houghton Mifflin Co., 1999. Two authors write different stories based on a similar incident.

Emberley, Ed. ***Ed Emberley's Drawing Book of Animals.*** Little Brown & Co., 1994 (reprint). One of many art books by the well-known author-illustrator with step-by-step directions for drawing a variety of critters.

Gee, Robyn. ***What Shall I Draw?*** EDC Publications, 1995. Step-by-step directions show how to draw a variety of items such as an owl, a rocket, and a dragon.

Hulme, Joy N. ***How to Write, Recite, and Delight in All Kinds of Poetry.*** Millbrook Press, 1996. Poems written by children are used as examples of various poetic forms.

Stevens, Janet. ***From Pictures to Words: A Book About Making a Book.*** Holiday House, 1995. A popular author-illustrator shows how she writes about and draws characters and settings to create a book.

Striker, Susan, with Edward Kimmel. ***The Anti-Coloring Book: Creative Activities for Ages 6 and Up.*** Owl Books, 2001. One of several books in a series that invite young artists to complete a drawing in a creative way.

Research Skills

Heiligman, Deborah. David Cain (illustrator). ***The Kid's Guide to Research.*** Scholastic Trade, 1999.

Souter, Gerry, Janet Souter, and Allison Souter. ***Researching on the Internet Using Search Engines, Bulletin Boards, and Listservs.*** Enslow Publishers, Inc., 2003.

Bookmaking

Diehn, Gwen. ***Making Books That Fly, Fold, Wrap, Hide, Pop Up, Twist, and Turn.*** Lark Books, 1998. Photographs and drawings show how to make a wide variety of books.

Valenta, Barbara. ***Pop-O-Mania: How to Create Your Own Pop-ups.*** Dial Books for Young Readers, 1997. Directions in three dimensions show readers how to create simple to complex pop-up books.

Getting Published

Henderson, Kathy. ***The Young Writer's Guide to Getting Published.*** Writers Digest Books, 2001 (6th edition).

Seuling, Barbara. ***To Be a Writer: A Guide for Young People Who Want to Write and Publish.*** Twenty-First Century Books, 1997.

Potluck: THE Magazine for the Serious Young Writer. A magazine that publishes work by young writers and artists. **www.potluck.org**

Stone Soup. A magazine that publishes work by young writers and artists. **www.stonesoup.com**

Word Dance. A magazine and website written for and by kids. **www.worddance.com.**

Zuzu. A magazine written and illustrated by children. **www.zuzu.org.**